Little Guide Book ASIAN LEAVES and ROOTS

Devagi Sanmugam
& Christopher Tan

Marshall Cavendish
Editions

This book contains previously published material from
Cooking with Asian Roots and Cooking with Asian Leaves

Copyright © 2014 Marshall Cavendish International (Asia) Private Limited

Published by Marshall Cavendish Cuisine
An imprint of Marshall Cavendish International

Limits of Liability/Disclaimer of Warranty: The Author and Publisher of this
book have used their best efforts in preparing this book. The Publisher
makes no representation or warranties with respect to the contents of this
book and is not responsible for the outcome of any recipe in this book.
While the Publisher has reviewed each recipe carefully, the reader may not
always achieve the results desired due to variations in ingredients, cooking
temperatures and individual cooking abilities. The Publisher shall in no event
be liable for any loss of profit or any other commercial damage, including but
not limited to special, incidental, consequential, or other damages.

Other Marshall Cavendish Offices:
99 White Plains Road, Tarrytown NY 10591-9001, USA • Marshall Cavendish
International (Thailand) Co Ltd. 253 Asoke, 12th Flr, Sukhumvit 21 Road,
Klongtoey Nua, Wattana, Bangkok 10110, Thailand • Marshall Cavendish
(Malaysia) Sdn Bhd, Times Subang, Lot 46, Subang Hi-Tech Industrial Park,
Batu Tiga, 40000 Shah Alam, Selangor Darul Ehsan, Malaysia

Marshall Cavendish is a trademark of Times Publishing Limited

National Library Board, Singapore Cataloguing-in-Publication Data

Devagi Sanmugam, author.
Asian leaves and roots / Devagi Sanmugam & Christopher Tan. – Singapore :
Marshall Cavendish Editions, [2014]
pages cm. – (Little guide book)
ISBN : 978-981-4561-30-3 (paperback)

1. Cooking, Asian. 2. Cooking (Vegetables) – Asia. 3. Root crops – Asia. I. Title.
II. Tan, Christopher, 1972-, author. III. Series: – Little guide book.

TX724.5.A1
641.595 -- dc23   OCN879137652

Printed in Singapore by Markono Print Media Pte Ltd

Contents

RECIPES

Introduction

On many occasions, we have seen shoppers examining vegetables and herbs with puzzled expressions, wondering what they are and how to cook them, and stallholders harassed by a queue of people wanting attention don't always have the time or disposition to answer questions! Leafy vegetables and knobbly root vegetables proliferate at vegetable stalls, in a wide array of shapes and sizes, scents and textures. Many are traditionally used by a particular culture, outside of which they are barely known. This book is intended to shed some light on those attractive bunches of leaves you liked the look of this morning but didn't recognise, the bag of herbs you bought last week and couldn't figure out a use for, and the knobbly, lumpen, soil-dusted shapes you found intriguing but didn't know how it can be prepared. It is not meant to be an exhaustive examination of every ingredient on the market, but a practical guide to using some of the herbs and root vegetables you may come across. We encourage you to quiz your vegetable seller, but a few samples, go home and experiment!

Agathi Leaves

Common West Indian pea tree,
White spinach (English), Daun turi (Malay),
Khae baan (Thai), Katuray (Tagalog),
Sua dua (Vietnamese)
Botanical Sesbania grandiflora

Agathi leaves are characterised by elongated oval light-green leaves grow close together in opposite pairs along a thin stalk, clustering together so they look a bit like giant mimosa. The crescent-shaped, cup-like flowers may be pink or white depending on the variety. Agathi leaves are usually sold in large bunches.

The slightly chewy leaves, similar to kale in their resilient texture, are tinged with bitterness. The bitter centres of the flowers are always removed before they are eaten.

Agathi leaves are well suited to being paired with coconut in the Indian fashion, whether with coconut milk in curries or with grated coconut in vegetable medleys, to contrast their bitter edge with natural sweetness. Stalks are always removed before cooking. In the Malay kitchen it is stir-fried, cooked in soups, curries or with coconut milk. In Malaysia and Thailand, the flowers are used in salads, and the Vietnamese add them to soups; they are treated as a vegetable in themselves in the Philippines, and they are either steamed or braised. Thai cooks stir-fry agathi leaves with meat or seafood, simmer their leaves in sour-spicy kaeng som curries, or blanch them and serve them with other cooked vegetables as accompaniments to nam prik relishes.

The bark, leaves and flowers of the sesbania tree are all used for medicinal purposes in different parts of the world, for conditions such as smallpox, dysentery and fevers. Agathi leaves, a good source of beta-carotene, protein and iodine, can be made into a tea with antibiotic and anti-cancer properties, and act as a diuretic and laxative in quantity. The bark and leaves can be pounded into a poultice for bruises and skin irritations, and the bark and leaves are juiced to make a mouthwash and gargle for sore throats.

Thai Sweet Basil

Common Daun selasih (Malay),
Luo le, Xiang cao (Chinese),
Bai horapa (Thai), Rau hung que
(Vietnamese)
Botanical Ocimum basilicum

The basil family is a large and diverse one, encompassing many different leaf shapes and sizes, colours, aromatic nuances, and potential culinary uses. The three most easily found in markets are Thai sweet basil, holy basil and lemon basil. A brief application of heat helps these different types of basil to release their full fragrance, holy basil most of all; many Thai dishes have whole or torn basil leaves stirred in at the very last minute before serving, allowing them just enough time to wilt and infuse the dish with their gorgeous perfume. Having said that, all three varieties marry superbly with salads, uncooked. Most of the goodness of Asian basils lies in their complexity when used fresh, so infusing them in oil or vinegar, as is done with basil in the west, is less culturally appropriate, though certainly possible.

***

Thai sweet basil has deep green leaves that are slightly less fragile and slightly more pointed than European sweet basil, with purplish stems and flowers. They smell just as sweet as European basil, but have hints of anise to their fragrance, and so are not simply interchangeable with the former.

Thai sweet basil has the broadest range of the three. With its aromatic sweetness, it is almost mild enough to be eaten as a vegetable, and it can be added to dishes in large quantities without overwhelming, and is used in stir-fried dishes, salads, soups and curries, where it rounds out the complex flavours of spice pastes beautifully.

Holy Basil

Common Hot basil,
Hairy basil (English),
Bai krapao (Thai), Tulsi (Hindi)
Botanical Ocimum sanctum,
Ocimum tenuiflorum

Holy basil leaves may be pale green with green stems (the more common kind in India and also called 'white' basil), or green with purple stems (more common in Thailand). They are covered with very fine hairs, and are smaller and more fragile than sweet basil leaves. Their heady aroma, like that of sweet basil overlaid with spicy notes of mint and clove, is only released in its full complexity when heat is applied, so it is added to dishes in the last stages of cooking.

Purple-stemmed holy basil is sharp and pungent and needs to be used more judiciously. 'White' holy basil is less strident. In Thai cuisine, both are typically added to stir-fried medleys of meat, seafood or vegetables, and can help to temper rich flavours. Minced pork fried with garlic, soy sauce and (authentically) enough chilli and holy basil to temporarily space you out is a classic Thai dish.

Of all the basils, holy basil is most closely associated with health-giving properties. Research has shown that it possesses antioxidant, anti-inflammatory, analgesic and anti-allergic qualities, helps to stabilise blood sugar levels and lower blood pressure, and primes the whole body to cope with and adapt to stress. It has long been used in Indian Ayurvedic medicine to relieve fevers.

Lemon Basil

Common Bai maenglak (Thai)
Botanical Ocimum citriodorum

Pale green and slightly fuzzy, Thai lemon basil has smaller and proportionately wider leaves than the sweet or holy varieties, and a distinctly lemony kick to its fragrance. It wilts quickly and overcooking makes it flat and characterless. It is more suited to the gentle bubble of curries or soups than the fierce heat of a wok, and so is used more for these kinds of dishes. It goes well with seafood.

It is the seeds of lemon basil that swell up with a jelly-like coating when soaked in water, and can then be used in desserts or drinks.

Sweet basil and lemon basil both aid digestion and relieve constipation. Thai herbalism prescribes basil for coughs, and uses the juice topically to heal skin irritations.

11

Boxthorn Leaves

Common Matrimony vine (English),
Gow gei (Cantonese), Gou qi (Chinese)
Botanical Lycium chinense,
lycium barbarum

Boxthorn has wide green leaves that should be removed from their stems very carefully, due to the short and very sharp thorns at the base of each leaf stalk. Sweet boxthorn fruit, or wolfberries (*kei chi* in Cantonese), frequently seen in Chinese herbal dishes, are sold dried in Chinese medicine shops and resemble small crimson raisins shaped like wrinkled rugby balls. It has a spinach-like flavour,

with a satisfying depth and slightly astringent aftertaste. Boxthorn is typically cooked and served in soup, or ample gravy, as it tastes too austere if served dry. It is classically combined with pork liver to make a nourishing soup. Another familiar sight on Cantonese menus is boxthorn cooked with eggs. A delicious way of cooking the leaves is to braise them in stock and topped with wolfberries that have been plumped briefly in hot oil.

In the Chinese food-as-medicine tradition, both boxthorn leaves and berries (which are high in carotene) are eaten to improve eyesight. The leaves and roots strengthen the muscles, liver and kidneys, clean the blood, and help to bring down fever and relieve thirst and coughs. Juice squeezed from the leaves is reputedly good for as an external treatment for mosquito bites. Boxthorn is a yin energy tonic that also promotes longevity.

Chives

Common Garlic chives (English),
Kuchai (Malay), Gau choy
(Cantonese), Jiu cai,
Jiu huang (Chinese)
Botanical Allium tuberosum

Across Asia, chives are found in
three forms: green chives, with
green, flat, slim-bladed leaves;
yellow chives, the same grown
in the dark; and flowering chives,
whose sturdier round leaves are
tipped by pointed pale green
buds, like little paintbrushes. All
three forms of Chinese chives have
a mild spring onion flavour, with
a garlicky hint; yellow chives have
a uniquely musky edge. All are

sweetest when young and slim, and fibrous and coarse-flavoured when too old.
They are also more pungent than Western onion chives (Allium schoenoprasum).

Green chives enliven dumpling fillings, *mee siam*, beef and seafood
preparations, and any dishes that benefit from their gentle but persistent onion-
garlic kick. They go well with smooth, subtle ingredients like eggs, bean curd
(tofu) and noodles. Flowering chives are most familiar when stir-fried as a
vegetable, often with seafood such as scallops or squid. They also stand up to
strong-flavoured meats, or organ meats like pork liver, a classic chive sidekick.
Fragile and perishable yellow chives are more suited to soups, steamed and
braised dishes; they should not be overcooked and combined with overbearing
flavours, or their delicate character will be lost.

In Chinese medicine, chives have various applications, particularly in
conditions affecting the stomach, liver, kidney and skin. They are warming, and
help to regulate energy flow and purify the blood. Chive seeds strengthen yang
energy and may be made into impotence remedies for men. The leaves can be
pulped or juiced then applied on rashes and skin ailments.

Chrysanthemum Leaves

Common Garland chrysanthemum,
Crown daisy (English), Tung hao
(Mandarin), Tong ho (Cantonese),
Sookgat (Korean), Tan o (Vietnamese),
Shungiku, Kikuna (Japanese)
Botanical Chrysanthemum coronarium
var. spatiosum

The common chrysanthemum coronarium varieties are the broad-leafed and small-leafed kinds. The latter has smaller and more deeply serrated leaves, whereas the former has round-edged leaves fanning out from long stalks. Both have a soft but resilient texture and are quite succulent after cooking. The small, densely-petalled flowers are usually yellow. Always choose young, fresh-looking greens with firm, juicy stems.

Chrysanthemum leaves have a faintly musky, pungent scent, with a distinctively tangy 'green' taste and a slight bitterness that increases as the leaves grow older. Small-leafed chrysanthemum is more pungent than the broad-leaf type. The edible flowers (not the same as those used for tea, which are chrysanthemum morifolii) are also slightly bitter.

Chinese, Japanese and Korean cuisines use the leaves in soups and steamboat dishes; rich stocks showcase their astringency better than thin broths. Very young leaves may be eaten raw, or blanched and used in salads, Japanese-style. They can also be stir-fried quickly or made into tempura. An easy way to prepare the leaves is to steam them briefly until just wilted and tender, and dress them with simple seasonings. They go well with sweet, nutty or rich ingredients, such as sesame oil and sesame paste, roasted garlic, sweetened miso, and so on. In Japan they might be combined with persimmons or an oil-rich seafood item. In Korea, they are quickly blanched and used to wrap meat and rice. Prolonged heating brings out a bitter flavour, so take care not to overcook them.

Culantro

Common Long coriander, Mexican coriander,
Sawtooth leaf (English), Ci yan sui (Chinese),
Ngo gai (Vietnamese), Pak chi farang (Thai),
Ketumbar jawa (Malay), Recao (Spanish)
Botanical Eryngium foetidum

Culantro has matte green, saw-edged leaves about 3–4 cm ($1^1/_4$–$1^1/_2$ in) wide and 20–25 cm (8–10 in) long, that spring directly from the base of the plant's central stem. They have a fleshy but resilient texture, similar to local lettuce leaves. The spiky flower heads are not eaten.

They are much like cilantro (coriander leaves) in scent and taste, but earthier and more blunt, with less subtlety and sweetness. Culantro roots likewise have a fragrance similar to cilantro roots. When dried, culantro retains more of its flavour than cilantro.

Culantro is native to Central America, hence its Spanish name—and also its Thai name, which literally translates as 'foreign coriander'—and there, it is often used to flavour salsas, beans, tomatoes, rice and meat dishes. It is also widely used across the Caribbean, often as a key ingredient in a sofrito, or sauce base, of aromatic herbs and vegetables.

In Vietnam, culantro is one of the many herbs eaten as standard accompaniments to an everyday meal. Hand-torn into shreds, it is essential as one of the toppings for pho bo, beef noodle soup. In Thailand, culantro is sometimes added to tom yam soups.

To clean culantro leaves, wipe them well with a damp cloth. Their matte surface sometimes carries dust and grit that a quick rinse may not remove.

Culantro is an adequate source of vitamins A, B2 and C. Its leaves and roots, eaten raw or made into a tea, have been used in folk medicine to treat stomach and digestive upsets, nausea and fevers. In Chinese and Indian medicine it is believed to dissipate wind and stimulate the stomach and appetite, and it is prescribed for colds in both China and the Caribbean.

Curry Leaves

Common Daun kari (Malay),
Karuvapillai (Tamil), Kari patta,
Meetha neem (Hindi), Bai karee (Thai)
Botanical Murraya koenigii

These diamond-shaped curry leaves are tough, bottle-green in colour and hang on very thin stems, forming almost feathery sprigs. A mature curry leaf tree bears white flowers and small black berries.

A scent warmly nuanced with pepper, green capsicum and citrus peel is released when the leaves are crushed or heated. To taste, the leaves are fleetingly acrid, but not unpleasantly so. Otherwise most of their character lie in their aroma.

A foundational spice in the cooking of south and coastal India and Sri Lanka, curry leaves are often found in the company of the other signature flavours of those regions, such as mustard seeds, ginger, coconut, chillies and onions. They are almost always fried in oil to bring out their fragrance, whether in the initial sautéing of spices for a dish, or in a *tarka*—a mixture of spices added into smoking hot oil, then stirred into a dish as the last step before serving. They add warm, peppery notes to chutneys and relishes, *sambars* (lentil and vegetable medleys) and *rasams* (aromatic sour broths drunk along with a meal).

In India, an infusion of curry leaves is given to relieve fevers, nausea, vomitting and intestinal discomfort. It is thought to be a liver-strengthener and blood purifier, with tonic, antibacterial, analgesic and antidysenteric qualities. Applied externally on the scalp in the form of an infused oil, and eaten in food, they are said to nourish the hair and slow down its greying. Curry leaves are among the herbs prescribed by both the Hindu Ayurvedic and Muslim Unani medical systems.

Daun Salam

Common Indonesian bay leaf (English)
Botanical Eugenia polyantha

Daun salam has dull green, slightly elongated leaves, about the size of a human palm. They turn brownish-green when dried.

A light herbal aroma with citrus notes distinguishes daun salam from European bay leaves, which have a totally different and much more assertive character.

Somewhat paradoxically, daun salam is not particularly strong in flavour or aroma and yet finds its way into many Indonesian dishes, where it contributes background notes rather than dominant ones. It is used to boost the fragrance of rice dishes, curry gravies, sambals, and steamed seafood or meat preparations, and it is usually added midway through cooking, or fried with other spices at the beginning.

Dill

Common Shi luo, Tu hui xiang (Chinese),
Adas cina (Malay), Pak chee lao (Thai),
Thi la (Vietnamese), Sowa (Hindi)
Botanical Anethum graveolens (Anethum sowa)

Dill foliage is bright bluish-green and feathery. The tiny flowers are yellow and grouped in circular heads. Dill seed is also used as a spice. The refreshing, unique scent of dill is reminiscent of caraway, flat-leaf parsley and anise. When dried, the plant's aroma becomes more concentrated and less sweet.

The Thai name for dill, *pak chi lao*, 'Laotian coriander', shows how important dill is to Laotian cuisine, where it flavours many cooked dishes. In northern Thailand, it is a frequent garnish, and in Vietnam, it appears in fish dishes, such as fish porridge, and Hanoi's *cha ca*, fried fish with rice noodles, peanuts and herbs. Dill also inevitably turns up in fish dishes across Scandinavia, as it counters the fattiness of oily fish like herring and salmon admirably, for example in *gravlaks*, salmon fillet cured in salt, sugar, white pepper, and liberal amounts of dill.

In both western and eastern European cuisine, cucumber has long been a traditional partner for dill, whether in a simple sliced cucumber salad dressed with chopped dill, or gherkin pickles made with herbed brine. Pungent as it is, dill is a good herb to infuse in vinegar (white wine, mild cider or rice vinegar work best) that you can then use for quick pickles, salad dressings or to perk up stews or barbecued meats. Dill also goes well with root vegetables like beetroot, potatoes and carrots, and also cabbage. It allies superbly with diary products such as sour cream, yoghurt, cream and curd cheeses, and butter, in dips, spreads, sauces and side dishes. Fresh or dried dill can be added to rye bread dough to enhance the sourness of rye in a delicious way.

A warming herb in Chinese medicine, dill is held to be good for the stomach and kidneys. An antibacterial agent (hence its popularity in pickling) and antispasmodic herb, It has been used for therapeutic purposes in India and the Middle East for many centuries. It aids digestion, dispels gas, freshens breath, encourages lactation in nursing mothers, and soothes colic; it is a key ingredient in gripewater, used to calm fractious babies, and in fact dill seed tea has been used for that exact purpose for several hundred years.

Drumstick Leaves

Common Merungai (Malay), Murungga keerai (Tamil), Malunggay (Filipino)
Botanical Moringa oleifera

Drumstick leaves are small and oval, attached to thin stems in small sprays. The leaves have a mild, sweet taste similar to pea shoots, with a slight warm bite, like cress. They can be eaten raw in salads when young, and otherwise stir-fried, steamed, or simmered in soups or curries; in all instances, cook them only just until tender, as overcooking leaches away their nutrients. Dried, they can be ground to a powder and added to dishes to boost their vitamin and protein content. Their subtle, pleasant flavour is as well suited to Western as Asian cooking—try sautéing them in butter or olive oil to serve with grilled or roasted meats, or adding them to stews.

The flowers are also edible, and the young pods, which taste a little like long beans and a little like asparagus, are a familiar sight in Indian curries and vegetable dishes. Considered a 'miracle tree' because of its many uses, fast growth and sturdiness—it has been used in anti-malnutrition programs in Third World countries—the drumstick tree is completely edible. The roots taste like horseradish, and the mature seeds can be roasted and eaten like nuts, sprouted, pressed for oil, or ground and used to purify water. The leaves have one of the highest protein counts of any vegetable, and containing several essential amino acids, they make an excellent addition to vegan diets. The young pods and leaves are also high in fibre. Drumstick leaves are rich in vitamins C and A, beta-carotene (more so than carrots), calcium (more so than cow's milk), iron (more so than spinach), potassium and other minerals. Because of their nutrients and their ability to encourage milk flow, they are a valuable tool for survival in impoverished countries where malnutrition threatens mothers and infants.

Fenugreek Leaves

Common Daun halba (Malay),
Hu lu ba cai (Chinese),
Methi saag (Hindi, Bengali),
Venthiya keerai (Tamil)
Botanical Trigonella foenum-graecum

Pea-green fresh fenugreek leaves are small, teardrop-shaped, and fan out in groups of three from slender stems. Only the leaves are eaten, as the stems are too bitter. Indian grocery stores in the tropics may store them in chiller cabinets because they will wilt easily in warm weather. Dried leaves (*kasoori methi* in Hindi) are dull olive-green in colour. Fenugreek seeds can also be sprouted like other herb seeds, to yield small cress-like shoots that can be eaten raw.

Refreshing nuances of celery, parsley, spinach and a distinct bitterness characterise the flavour and aroma of fenugreek leaves, which work to stimulate the appetite. Cooking mellows their bitterness but does not eradicate it.

The flavour of the leaves is strongest when eaten raw in salads, but may be too pronounced for palates unfamiliar with its charms. In Indian cuisine, and especially in northern India, where they are considered a delicacy, they are prepared in many ways: simmered until they collapse into a thick purée; chopped and used to stuff flatbreads and fritters; dried, crumbled and added to wafers, snacks, vegetable stews and gravies; cooked with lentils; or simply steamed. They partner starchy ingredients like wheat and potatoes well.

Some bitterness, but also some flavour, can be removed by blanching fenugreek leaves in boiling water, then rinsing them in cold water, before using them further in a recipe. Fenugreek sprouts may be treated just like other sprouts like alfalfa and cress, eaten in sandwiches and salads or added at the last minute to a stir-fry.

Gotu Kola

Common Indian pennywort (English),
Ji xue cao (Chinese), Daun pegaga (Malay),
Bai bua bok (Thai), Rau ma (Vietnam)
Botanical Centella asiatica

The leaves are kidney shaped, with slightly scalloped edges, and are carried by long, fleshy stalks. The flowers are pink. Raw, they have a strong grassy-herbal flavour with a bittersweet aftertaste. They are more often eaten raw than cooked.

Finely shredded gotu kola leaves may be eaten raw in salads or *kerabu* dishes. Because of its bitterness, it is often mixed with other leaves. In Malaysia and Vietnam, it is also made into a bright green, sweetened cold drink; in Vietnam, it is sometimes included in the herb plate present at every meal, and also made into soups. In Thai cuisine, it is added to salads, or eaten as part of raw vegetable platters, and Thai kickboxers drink gotu kola tea to speed up the healing of their bruises!

Gotu kola is far more strongly associated with medicinal recipes than culinary ones. It has long been a very important herb in folk medicine traditions all over the world, from Indian and Chinese to Indonesian, Papua New Guinean and Thai. Rich in vitamins, minerals and bioactive compounds, it reputedly shows antioxidant, antibacterial, antiviral, and anti-inflammatory activity; strengthens circulation, digestion and metabolism; rejuvenates the nervous system, mental function and memory; increases longevity; heals all manner of skin ailments, from burns and wounds to leprosy and psoriasis; is a diuretic and blood-purifier; brings down fevers and high blood pressure; and has many other qualities, hence its status as a 'one-herb pharmacy'.

Perhaps the most important roles of gotu kola in modern medicine is as a treatment for skin irritations, as it has a remarkable ability to help skin cells regenerate and knit together, and as a natural remedy for the different forms of arthritis and other conditions caused by inflamed tissues.

Kaffir Lime Leaves

Common Kaffir lime leaf, Leprous lime leaf
(English), Daun limau purut (Malay),
Daun jeruk purut (Bahasa Indonesia),
Bai makrut (Thai), Krauch soeuch (Cambodia)
Botanical Citrus hystrix

The double-lobed leathery leaves are glossy dark green on their upper side and matte pale green on their undersides, with a thick central vein. Stalks are tough and thorny. Unlike many other herbs, the leaves freeze very well if packed flat in resealable bags. When sliced or crushed, the leaves emit a powerful balsam-citrus fragrance that quickly perfumes any dish.

Kaffir lime leaves are especially important ingredients in Thai, Indonesian, Malay and Cambodian kitchens. Because of their potency they are used as a flavouring or garnish rather than a main ingredient; they are typically torn up to better release their aroma, or shredded hair-fine if they are to be eaten. Beef *rendang*, tom yam soup, fish cakes and *otak ot*, *yu sheng* and *nasi ulam* would all be unthinkable without the scent of kaffir lime!

Although they go well with almost any meat, the leaves' invigorating spicy freshness makes them a natural partner for seafood, especially shellfish. They can also lighten the heaviness of coconut-based dishes, as their presence in *rendang* and other curries illustrates. In Cambodia, they are pounded into many different kinds of *kroeung*, or spice paste. Deep-fried until crisp, the leaves make a good garnish for meat dishes; combined with deep-fried chillies and garlic, they frequently appear in Thai snacks.

Many recipes require lime leaves to be cut into hair-fine slivers; the easiest way to do this is to remove the leaves' thick veins, stack the leaf blades neatly, and then slice them with a heavy and very sharp knife.

Laksa Leaves

Common Daun kesum (Malay)
Botanical Polygonum minus

Laksa leaves have small, pointed, thin green leaves, growing out on thin but strong stems. They has a faintly sour taste, with a delightful clean, lemony aroma reminiscent of turmeric leaves, cilantro, sorrel and lemon basil.

In Malaysia, laksa leaves are best known as an aromatic garnish for laksa, a spicy noodle dish, as well as a main player in *nasi kerabu* and *nasi ulam*, and an essential element in many dishes combining seafood and tamarind, such as Penang *assam laksa*, *assam pedas* and *udang nenas*.

In Thailand and Vietnam, *rau ram* is used in salads, often lavishly. Its fragrance is able to lift and enhance other citrus aromas in a dish, and temper the richness of meat and seafood. In combination with other herbs and spices, it stimulates the appetite wonderfully.

Laksa leaves wilt quickly after being removed from their stems, and even quicker once they are cut, so ideally prepare them just before use.

According to traditional Malay medicine, it is a warming herb that is good for the eyesight. Ongoing research in Malaysia suggests that it may contain useful antioxidants. Its botanical relative, Polygonum multiflorum or *he shou wu*, is well known in China as a potent yin tonic, beneficial for the liver, kidneys and blood.

Noni Leaves

Common Indian mulberry, Morinda (English), Daun mengkudu, Daun mengkudu besar (Malay), Hai ba ji, Wu ning, Luo ling (Chinese), Yo baan (Thai), Nha u (Vietnamese)
Botanical *Morinda citrifolia*

Noni leaves are large, leathery and slightly glossy, varying in colour from pale to deep green.

The leaves have a faint scent not unlike that of spinach, and a mild and very slightly bitter taste somewhat like grass and screwpine (pandan) leaf. They have a dry, tough texture unless they are very young.

Noni leaves are an important herb in the traditional *ulam* cuisine of Malaysia, featuring for example in the Kelantanese rice salad *khau jam,* otherwise known as *nasi kerabu*. For this dish, rice is cooked in the squeezed juice of a large assortment of herbs, and then has more fresh sliced herbs stirred in before serving. Finely shredded to make them easier to chew, they may be stir-fried with other vegetables, fried rice or noodles, or cooked in a sambal. In Indonesian cuisine, they are often cooked with coconut, in *urap* vegetable dishes, steamed in banana leaf in pepes fashion, or in *gulai* gravies. In the Pacific Islands, noni leaves are used to wrap fish before they are roasted or steamed.

Noni leaves, which do contain antioxidants, vitamins and many bioactive compounds, can be boiled to make a tonic drink, or pounded and spread on irritated skin to calm it; Malay herbal tradition dictates that heated leaves can be put on the chest to soothe coughs and nausea, and in the West Indies and Polynesia, the same is done for aches and pains in muscles and joints. Tongans and other Pacific Islanders infuse noni flowers to make an eyewash.

Paku

Common Vegetable fern (English),
Paku, Pucuk paku, Paku benar (Malay),
Pakis (Bahasa Indonesia), Phak kuut (Thai)
Botanical Diplazium esculentum,
athyrium esculentum

Paku are typically sold in bundles of feathery, light green fronds about 40 cm (16 in) long. You may find a few closely related species and subspecies of ferns in each bundle, distinguished only by slight differences in leaf shape. Only the youngest, most tender leaves and stems are eaten. Paku ferns are mild in flavour. The thickest, most succulent stems have a taste reminiscent of young asparagus.

Paku ferns are eaten widely throughout the Philippines, Malaysia, Thailand, Papua New Guinea, and other Pacific Islands. In Malay cuisine, they are eaten in *kerabu* dishes, cooked in coconut milk gravy, or stir-fried with sambal — one popular variation includes dried and sometimes fresh prawns plus hot chillies. They may also be simply eaten plain with sambal *belacan*. A well known *urap* dish in Indonesia combines ferns with grated coconut, spices and bean sprouts.

Fiddleheads, the tightly curled heads of another fern species, are enjoyed as a delicacy in North America; they are paired with rich sauces, puréed into soups, or cooked in butter and served as a side dish. These are treatments that could also suit Asian paku.

Before use, always sort ferns thoroughly, removing any brown, dry or soggy fragments, then wash well and drain. Thick, woody stems or overly tough leaves should be picked out and discarded. When raw, they can sometimes be bitter, so it may help to blanch them briefly first if they are not to be cooked further in your recipe.

Rice Paddy Herb

Common Rau om, Ngo om (Vietnamese),
Ma om (Khmer), Pak kayang (Thai)
Botanical Limnophila aromatica

The rice paddy herb has small
spear-shaped leaves with slightly
serrated edges. They are lime
green in hue, and are borne by
fleshy, thick, fuzzy stems. The tiny
flowers are trumpet-shaped and
lavender-coloured.

It has a unique and complex
fragrance, combining elements of
jasmine, celery, cinnamon, cumin
and citrus, not unlike shiso, but
with a 'soapy' edge.

Rice paddy herb finds its principal uses in Vietnamese cuisine, where it is
invariably used raw as a garnish or topping. The floral, herbal, spicy and fresh
notes in its perfume enable it to harmonise well with sweet, sour, fruity and
spiced dishes. It is notably added to *canh chua*, sweet and sour fish soup, and
curries, and may even be used to garnish fresh fruit platters. Khmer cooks also
add rice paddy herb to several kinds of dishes, like stews, soups and congee; as
in Vietnam, it frequently accompanies fish and seafood.

Shiso

Common Shiso, Ohba (Japanese),
Beefsteak plant, Japanese mint (English),
Ta tio (Vietnamese), Nga kee mon (Thai),
Kkaennip (Korean)
Botanical Perilla frutescens

About 10–15 cm (4–5 in) long,
serrated-edged shiso leaves taper off
from a broad base. They have well-
defined veins and are covered with
a fine fuzz of leaf hairs. The colours
of different cultivars vary from vivid
green (*ao-shiso*) to deep purple-red
(*aka-shiso*). Fresh and sweet, with
a slightly astringent bite; the young
leaves of shiso sprouts have a definite spiciness. Shiso has a uniquely heady
aroma with hints of mint, parsley and celery; but this quickly dissipates when
the herb is heated, so shiso should be used raw or barely cooked.

Shiso is most commonly seen in sushi bars as a verdant garnish for
sashimi, but the Japanese have many other uses for it. In *sumiyaki* (charcoal-
grilled cuisine), green shiso may be used to wrap or fill pork and fish, with
its freshness used as a counterpoint to oily, rich flavours. Red shiso leaves are
added to pickled plums (*umeboshi*) and pickled ginger to dye them an intense
pink; a popular home-style dish flavours cooked rice with minced *umeboshi* and
shredded green shiso leaves. Red shiso flower heads are also used as a sashimi
and sushi condiment. Shiso extract also features in commercial beverages and
food products. Korean cooks also use shiso leaves that are larger and milder-
flavoured than their Japanese cousins in many dishes. They are made into kimchi
and pickles, used to wrap cooked foods such as grilled meat, and are added to
pancakes, soups and salads.

Red shiso leaves number among the wide selection of herbs omnipresent
on the Vietnamese table. They are used to garnish noodle dishes, stews or salads
or simply eaten along with the daily meal.

Slippery Vegetable

Common Malabar spinach,
Indian spinach, Ceylon spinach,
Vine spinach, Slippery spinach (English),
Hua cai, Teng cai (Chinese), San choy
(Cantonese), Pasala keerai (Tamil),
Poi (Hindi), Remayong (Malay),
Pak plung (Thai)
Botanical Basella alba (Green variety),
Basella rubra (Red variety)

This is a vibrant green vine plant with
succulent stems and broad, rounded,
perky leaves. Usually only the young
leaves and stems are harvested for
eating; they have a slightly rubbery
feel to them. The red-leafed type
turns green during cooking. A closely related species also eaten in China, Basella
cordifolia, has heart-shaped leaves.

The distinguishing feature of this green, as its name suggests, is its slightly
mucilaginous quality when cooked, similar to lady's finger. Its pleasant, earthy
flavour is reminiscent of spinach and pea shoots.

In Asia, it is most commonly used in soups. Slippery vegetable can also
be stir-fried, blanched or braised successfully, provided cooking times are kept
short; the longer you cook it, the slimier it gets. However, this quality can also be
used to thicken soup or gravies slightly. Very young leaves may be eaten raw in
salads. In northern Thailand, slippery vegetable is added to curries, and in India,
it is cooked in similar ways to spinach.

Slippery vegetable is a good source of vitamins A and C, calcium and zinc.
Chinese and Indian medicine consider it good for constipation and intestinal
complaints: crushed, the leaves can be used as a poultice for burns, boils and
skin ailments. In parts of Thailand and India, it is also deemed good for the
kidneys. All three countries classify it as a cooling vegetable.

Sweet Potato Leaves

Common Daun ubi keledek (Malay),
Fan shu (Chinese), Vathalang-kelengu
(Tamil), Fun-shu (Cantonese)
Botanical Ipomoea batatas

These soft green heart-shaped leaves are the size of a human palm, with juicy stems. It has a mild, spinach-like flavour. The stems are pleasingly succulent when cooked until just tender. The bland juiciness of these leaves means that they go well with strong flavours, hence the popularity of *sambal daun ubi keledek*. In Africa, they may be cooked with other vegetables in a medley seasoned with smoked fish and hot chillies.

Some varieties have been cultivated to be rich sources of protein and calcium. According to Chinese medicinal lore, sweet potato leaves are good for soothing stomachache and intestinal discomfort, and help the lungs and renal system to function properly.

Turmeric Leaves

Common Daun kunyit (Malay),
Jiang huang cai (Chinese)
Botanical Curcuma domestica

Feather-shaped and pointed, with distinct striations, light green turmeric leaves can grow to be 30–45 cm (12–18 in) long. They are lime green in colour, and are similar to a feather in its striations and long, pointed dimensions. They a very mild grassy taste, and a lemony scent that is light but enticing. It calls to mind the most volatile gingery, citrusy notes of the aroma of cut turmeric root.

Turmeric leaves are an omnipresent herb in Malay and Indonesian cooking. It is a must in the rice and herb salads *nasi ulam* and *nasi kerabu*. It is less assertive than the other herbs in the dishes, such as ginger bud and kaffir lime leaf, but it provides a valuable and subtle background aroma that reinforces the similar scent of laksa leaf. In Sumatra, turmeric leaves are often added to *masak lemak* dishes and curries, such as *rendang*, where they help to balance out the richness of coconut milk and meat juices. Turmeric leaves are also used to flavour fish soups and stews. In Thailand, they are stirred into fish soups with other aromatic herbs. They go well with seafood, and may be shredded and stirred into *otak* or fishcake mixtures before cooking, for example. Whole leaves may be used to wrap large pieces of fish before they are grilled, steamed or fried; a special southern Vietnamese dish rolls pieces of marinated eel in turmeric leaves before charcoal-grilling them.

Turmeric leaves are treasured more for their culinary potential, as opposed to the turmeric root, which has long been revered in India for its wide spectrum of healing properties and applications. However, oil extracted from turmeric leaves also has antibacterial qualities.

Watercress

Common Xi yang cai (Chinese),
Sai yeung choi (Cantonese),
Semanggi (Malay), Selada air
(Bahasa Indonesia)
Botanical Nasturtium officinale,
Rorippa nasturtium-acquaticum

Watercress has fleshy, thick pale green stems with small, widely-spaced oval leaves of a slightly darker green. Rootlets may sprout from the main stem. The flowers are white.

Raw, watercress has a crisp earthiness and a slightly biting mustardy, peppery edge. Cooked, the leaves fade to a dull olive green and loses its pungency, but acquires a velvety texture and pleasant vegetable flavour.

In Chinese cuisine, watercress is most often braised or boiled in soups, for instance with pork ribs. It may also be stir-fried. In the West, it is also a classic soup ingredient, usually combined with potato, but is also often eaten raw in salads. Its punchy flavour combines well with sweet or tangy ingredients such as citrus fruit, apples and pears, and makes a good foil to rich ingredients such as avocado, mayonnaise, oily fish and cheese. Watercress sandwiches on lightly buttered bread are an English high-tea tradition, and a sprig of watercress is a time-honoured garnish for steak and game. It makes an excellent addition to egg dishes, such as scrambled eggs, omelettes and quiches.

Cut off the roots and thickest lower part of watercress stems before washing well and using.

Watercress is rich in vitamins A, B and C, as well as calcium, iron and other minerals. Its raw juices stimulate the appetite, and also have a diuretic effect. Research suggests that it also has anti-cancer properties, as do other vegetables in the Cruciferae family that it belongs to.

Wild Pepper Leaves

Common Wild pepper, Betel pepper,
Wild betel (English), Daun kadok
(Malay), La lot (Vietnamese),
Bai cha phluu (Thai), Jia ju (Chinese)
Botanical Piper sarmentosum

The dark green, heart-shaped leaves
are glossy and intricately veined. Thin
and springy, they grow thickly on their
vine, hence the plant's popularity as
ground cover along roadsides and in
parks. They are frequently confused
with betel leaves (piper betel), which
are somewhat paler, less glossy and
longer in shape.

A peppery, herbal aroma, and
slightly tangy and sometimes faintly
bitter taste make wild pepper leaves a good complement to rich or meaty
ingredients. They are best eaten when no bigger than the size of a human palm.

Wild pepper is one of the herbs used in *ulam* dishes in northern Malaysia,
and southern Thailand. Its gentle heat helps to wake up the palate and prime
it for other flavours. *Thit bo nuong la lot* is a classic, beautifully subtle Vietnamese
dish, part of the seven-course beef banquet called *bo bay mon*. It features
spiced minced beef wrapped in wild pepper leaves, grilled to yield a dark and
fragrant crust.

The Thai dish *miang kum* wraps finely cut ingredients that may include
dried shrimp, lime flesh, roasted coconut, shallots, chillies, peanuts and diced
ginger, in wild pepper leaves with a sweet-sour sauce and folds them into one-
bite bundles. Street vendors typically sell sticks holding three or four neatly-
shaped *miang kum* for hungry passersby to snack on, and also take-home DIY
kits with sachets of all the ingredients, sauce and a stack of leaves. Wild pepper
leaves are also added to some Thai curries and seafood dishes, for example *pla
kung*, marinated prawns.

Beetroot

Common Tian cai gen (Mandarin),
Ubi bit (Malay), Beetroot kilangu (Tamil),
Chukandar (Hindi), Biito (Japanese)
Botanical Beta vulgaris

Beets come in a whole spectrum of colours—red, pink, red-black, gold, peachy yellow and striped red and white. They also vary considerably in shape and size, from tiny, teardrop-like to cylindrical to heftily rotund. Most common in Asian markets, however, are beets shaped like fat teardrops, about the size of a large fist, with deep burgundy-hued flesh. Very occasionally, one might come across fresh or preserved baby beets, the size of large marbles. Choose beets that are heavy and free of soft spots. If their tops are still on, look for lively, non-limp green leaves, an indicator of freshness. Avoid those with dried-out leaves or excessive hairy rootlets.

Red beets have the deepest, most mouth-filling flavour of all beets, combining sweetness with a gently earthy, sometimes mineral edge; the damp-earth flavour specifically comes from a compound called geosmin. Beet greens have a slightly metallic, slightly medicinal flavour that is an acquired taste. Texturally, young beets have the most pleasing crunch when raw, but all beets can be braised into melting softness.

Keep beets in the refrigerator's vegetable drawer, individually wrapped in plastic. Use them soon after purchase for the best results. To prevent beets from leaking juice everywhere, scrub them and cook them with their skins on; do not cut through the skin at all. For the most concentrated, sweetest flavour, wrap beets in foil and roast them at 180°C (350°F) for about an hour or so, until tender—the skins will easily rub and peel off. For quicker cooking, steam whole beets over high heat for 20–25 minutes.

Because of their sweetness and their unique character, which is easygoing but also hard to overshadow, beets get along equally well with rich, spicy, fruity, acidic and even bitter flavours. However, they do not blend well with strong fermented or fishy flavours.

Coarsely grate or julienne raw beets and dress them with a vinaigrette of balsamic vinegar and olive oil or, better, hazelnut or walnut oil. Try using beets in mixed salads with such fruit as fresh apricots, apples and oranges, and nutty or bitter vegetables like rocket, radicchio, fennel, frisée, endive and watercress. Raw beetroot juice can be mixed with other vegetable or fruit juices. Create new and unusual side dishes with slices or chunks of roasted

beets by giving a light drizzle of olive oil and topping with a salty or pungent ingredient, such as crumbly feta cheese, a trickle of seasoned yellow or mellow barley miso and finely minced Indian lime pickle or salted preserved lemons; or simply top with lime juice, lime zest and sea salt.

Take a tip from eastern European traditions and simmer grated or cubed beets in a clear meat or vegetable stock to make borscht, which can be translucent and light (and served cold), or made chunky and ribsticking with lots of meat and vegetables. Do not forget the sour cream on the side as beets have an unexpected affinity with tangy dairy products, such as sour cream, crème fraîche and yoghurt. Beetroot is also a popular vegetable in south and southeastern India, where it is made into chutneys, vadais (fritters), rasam (appetiser broths) and halwa (a sweet confection).

The deep scarlet pigments that give red beets their colour, betalains, are also antioxidants; the principal one is betanin. Beetroot is also a good source of vitamins C and A, minerals and folate. Raw beet juice or very lightly cooked beets (in broth or soup) are the best ways to exploit its nutritional benefits, although not necessarily the most delicious.

Burdock

Common Niu bang zi (Mandarin),
Gobo (Japanese)
Botanical Arctium lappa

Burdock roots can grow up to around 1 metre in length, so they are usually sold chopped into more manageable sections. Choose those no thicker than 3 cm (1^1/$_4$ in) across. Their skins range from dark beige to tan and, a bit like parsnips, are irregularly marked with faint ridges and spots. The flesh underneath is a dirty-cream colour and sticky when sliced. It also darkens very quickly when exposed to air.

Burdock has some of the sweetness of carrot but is not nearly as versatile. Its flavour is distinctly earthy and mineral and has been compared to that of artichoke, a distant relative. To some palates, burdock is faintly tinged with bitterness and, in short, can be something of an acquired taste. Pickled or cooked for a short while, it has a pleasingly resilient crunch. Cooked for longer periods, it achieves tenderness but loses some of its character.

Keep burdock wrapped in a brown paper bag, in the refrigerator's vegetable drawer. Use it up within a few days. There is no real need to peel burdock and, in fact, much of its flavour lies just under the skin, which is no thicker than carrot skin. Just wash it to get rid of caked dirt and trim any bruised parts.

Cut burdock turns brown astonishingly quickly. Although this process is slightly slowed by soaking the cut root in salted water or water acidulated with lemon juice or vinegar, the browning is inevitable and, thus, not worth stressing about. A soak of 15 minutes or more in cold water also helps to tame burdock's bitterness. Clean and cut burdock immediately before cooking to preserve flavour and nutrients.

A classic Japanese home-cooked dish is burdock *kinpira*—matchsticks of the root fried and then simmered with sesame oil, soy sauce, sake, sugar and crushed dried chilli, which all enhance burdock's woodsy flavour. Another simple home-style dish is made by lightly bruising blanched burdock, then marinating it in seasoned vinegar; this makes a good accompaniment to rich, meat-based main dishes. The Japanese also enjoy *gobo misozuke*, burdock that has been pickled in crocks of miso paste for several months.

Shredded burdock can be stir-fried with minced or thinly sliced meat and seasoned simply with soy sauce and sake for a quick dish. For variation, simmer burdock batons in water or light stock until tender, then add to composed vegetable salads, pilafs of rice or other grains, mixed-vegetable gratins, or casseroles.

Burdock contains inulin, a soluble fibre that tastes slightly sweet but has little effect on blood sugar levels as it is largely indigestible. However, it can give some people gas, if consumed in large amounts.

In Chinese medicine, burdock is considered a detoxifying food that dissipates heat. In olden times, grated burdock or burdock-cooking water was used in English folk medicine as a wash for skin afflictions.

Cassava

Common Tapioca (Asian English), Mu shu
(Mandarin), Ubi kayu (Malay), Maravalli kilangu
(Tamil), Simla alu (Hindi), Kamoteng kahoy
(Tagalog), Man sampalang (Thai), Manioc,
Yuca, Mandioca (Latin America)
Botanical Manihot esculenta

Cassava roots are shaped like giant, stubby carrots about 5 cm (2 in) across and 20–30 cm (8–12 in) long. Their rough skins, which may vary in colour from pale to dark brown, look and feel like thin tree bark. Ultra-fresh roots begin with slightly glossy skins that become dustier and greyer as they age. Beneath the skin is a thin, pinkish underlayer that should be peeled away with the skin to reveal the root's white or pale ivory flesh.

A most elegant vegetable, cassava develops a starchy smoothness when cooked and a subtly sweet, almost buttery flavour, sometimes with nuances of almond and new potato. It is best eaten warm as it can become waxen and solid when cold. Fortunately, it reheats obediently.

Cassava is sometimes sorted into 'sweet' and 'bitter' categories. These may reflect genetic differences or growing conditions, or both. Bitter cassava, more common to Africa than Asia, is more toxic than sweet cassava and requires more processing—soaking and repeated boilings—to render it fully edible. The bitterness comes from cyanide compounds, which are present in all cassava at some level. Hence, raw cassava must never be eaten as it can cause severe reactions.

Keep cassava roots at cool room temperature, in a well-ventilated place away from direct sunlight. They should be used within a few days of purchase. Before use, trim off the bark and underlayer from cassava root sections with a small, sharp knife. After or before cooking, it may be necessary to remove the thin, fibrous core that runs through the centre of the root.

Here in Southeast Asia, we are most familiar with cassava in the form of fried patties of grated or mashed cassava: cassava chips; fermented cassava tapé; and the innumerable *kuih-kuihs* made from different permutations of cassava and coconut, including *kuih bingka* (baked grated cassava cake). Variations of the lattermost are found in the Philippines and across the Pacific. The Thais serve syrup-simmered cassava with glutinous rice and coconut cream and the Peranakans (Straits Chinese) *pengat ubi kayu* (cassava cooked in sweetened coconut milk).

Cassava can also be cooked to accompany more western-style dishes too. Steam or boil it until tender, then mash it into a delicious purée with milk or stock; add more liquid to turn it into soup. Cut cassava into batons, steam or boil, then dress with garlic butter; a simple vinaigrette; or even just salt, olive oil and chilli flakes.

There is much also to learn from African and Caribbean kitchens, which abound in original preparations of this important staple. In central Africa, cassava pieces are cooked in water or broth, then stirred and pounded until they disintegrate into a smooth, sticky side dish called fufu; baton de manioc is another side dish made by wrapping pounded raw cassava pulp in leaves and steaming it for a long time. Jamaicans grate cassava into moist pulp, squeeze it dry, then shape it into small patties that are then cooked on a hot griddle to make bammy cakes, typically eaten with fried fish. In the West Indies, cassava juice is simmered with sugar and spices to make a syrup called cassareep, which is used to thicken a meat stew called pepperpot.

In Brazil, coarsely ground dried cassava, called farinha de mandioca, is mixed with oil or butter and fried over low heat until fragrant to make farofa, an ubiquitous condiment that accompanies many different dishes. In Asia, cassava starch (usually labelled 'tapioca flour') is widely used in sweet and savoury dishes, doughs and batters as a binding agent. It produces clear, glossy sauces and is especially good for thickening glazes for fruit-covered tarts or cakes.

Elephant Yam

Common Elephant's foot yam, Bai ban mo,
Chou mo yu, Zhong bao mo yu (Mandarin),
Senai kilangu (Tamil), Suran, Zaminkand
(Hindi), Pungapung (Tagalog)
Botanical Amorphophallus paeoniifolius

As its name suggests, elephant yam is a hefty tuber, shaped like a lumpy, squashed sphere. Some have likened its appearance to an UFO! It ranges in size and typically measures between 20 cm (8 in) and 40 cm (16 in) across. The smallest commercial specimens are about the size of small heads of broccoli and weigh upwards of 500 g (1 lb 1^1/$_2$ oz). It is often sold in markets still half-coated in mud and earth. Under the dark, crusty skin is pretty, apricot-hued flesh.

A wild African yam (Dioscorea elephantipes) is also called elephant's foot yam but it is comparatively rare in Asia. Furthermore, its tubers can weigh up to 300 kg so it is unlikely to be confused with the variety featured here. Konnyaku yams are sometimes confusingly called elephant yams.

Despite its unusual appearance, elephant yam is bland when cooked, so take care to season it well. It has an unusual, slightly milky aroma, almost like hot cereal, and a moist, cottony texture.

Keep elephant yams in a cool, well-ventilated place away from direct sunlight. To remove the skin, it is easiest to cut the washed yam into large pieces with a cleaver first, and then cut away the skin with a small sharp knife.

In southern India, many subtly different preparations for this yam exist—braised with aromatics and just a little water to make a dry curry; simmered with green banana, coconut, yoghurt and spices to make a *kaalan* curry; and combined with various other vegetables and coconut in a tangy aviyal curry. It can also be pressure-cooked with dhal and puréed, then seasoned with oil-tempered spices or mashed, seasoned and shaped into round balls that are then deep-fried to make elephant yam *bonda.*

When stewing elephant yam chunks, deep-fry them briefly to give them a thin crust and lightly caramelised flavour. They can also be steamed until cooked, then sautéed with crushed garlic in butter until golden for a basic side dish.

When mashed, elephant yam has a consistency much like potato, and so can be substituted for it in, patties, croquettes, dosa fillings, pie toppings, and so on. For an especially smooth purée to serve as a side dish, blend two parts elephant yam with one part white sauce and season with pepper and a dash of mustard.

NOTE: This is a true yam, containing oxalic acid crystals that may irritate the skin upon contact. Wear gloves when preparing it to avoid this risk; traditionally, cooks rubbed their hands and knives with cooking oil. Some people who are allergic to true yams may feel a prickling sensation in their throats when they eat them.

Konnyaku

Common Devil's tongue, Devil's root,
Mo yu (Mandarin), Konnyaku ver (Tamil)
Botanical Amorphophallus konjac

Konnyaku tubers are large, lumpy, irregular and earthy brown in colour. Few people ever see them, however, as they are too troublesome to process at home. Konnyaku jelly is the most common form in which it is sold and to make it, the root is first peeled, sliced, dried and crushed. The resulting powder is then dissolved in water, left to stand and coagulated with the help of alkaline lime. Lastly, the gel is cut into rectangular slabs, which may then be boiled to firm up their texture or, occasionally, frozen to make them more spongy. Konnyaku jelly does not melt like gelatin or agar-agar and is stable enough to be served hot.

Usually sold vacuum-packed in water, commercial konnyaku jelly is sometimes labelled 'alimentary paste' and comes in a few different grades and shades—from dark grey (often speckled with bits of black hijiki seaweed) to a lighter pearl-grey and white; the lighter it is, the more refining the starch has gone through before being made into gel. Other forms of commercial konnyaku include noodles—the thicker ones are called ito-konnyaku and the thinner, paler type *shirataki*—and, more rarely, nuggets shaped like tubes, flattened discs, commas or other shapes that seem to mimic seafood.

Konnyaku is a textural food. All of its processed forms have the springy consistency—as firm as agar-agar, but bouncier—that is unique to the tuber's glucomannan fibre. Konnyaku has a slightly fishy smell, which will be obvious as soon as you open a packet, but it dissipates after a few rinsings. Cooking also eliminates any fishiness. Its flavour is bland, faintly earthy and, frankly, not very remarkable.

Keep all kinds of konnyaku refrigerated and abide by their use-by dates. If you want to serve konnyaku without further cooking, such as in salads or cold dishes, you can firm it up by parboiling for a few minutes or by rubbing it with salt, then letting it stand before rinsing well; this is not necessary if you plan to braise or simmer it. Konnyaku noodles should be rinsed with boiling or very hot water before use.

'Sliced or cubed konnyaku is often braised or stewed with assorted meats and/or vegetables, chosen to give the resulting dish a pleasing gamut of textures and colours. One such is Japanese *oden*—assorted broth-simmered items, which include fishcake, taro, daikon, carrot and tofu.

While shirataki and other konnyaku noodles are well suited to being eaten cold as a savoury item or a dessert, they also make an intriguing alternative to wheat or rice noodles in hot soups, especially meat-based ones. Bundles of shirataki are a key part of traditional

Clockwise from top, left: grey ito-konnyaku; moulded konnyaku nuggets; shirataki; and on large plate: dark hijiki-flecked konnyaku, pale grey konnyaku and white konnyaku.

Japanese *sukiyaki* and can also be used in other Asian dishes, such as a Thai *yam woon sen* (mung-bean vermicelli) salad or a Korean *chap chae* (noodle stir-fry); or dress them with a northern Chinese sauce of chopped raw garlic, black vinegar, soy sauce and shredded leek.

Powdered konnyaku is used as a gelling agent in Asia to make firm-textured, crystal-clear dessert jellies. Instead of water and flavouring, consider using other liquids as a base for konnyaku jellies, such as unsweetened fruit juice, coconut water or wine.

The particular kind of dietary fibre found in konnyaku, glucomannan, is known to be an excellent remedy for constipation. Research suggests that it also helps to lower cholesterol levels and may encourage proper regulation of blood sugar levels in diabetic patients. Because it passes through the system largely undigested, konnyaku has a calorie count of almost zero.

Lotus Root

Common Lian ou (Mandarin), Teratai (Malay),
Tamarai ver (Tamil), Kamal (Hindi), Renkon,
Hasu (Japanese), Bua luang (Thai)
Botanical Nelumbo nucifera

Lotus roots are actually rhizomes, or swollen stems from which the roots grow, and are shaped like sausage links, with ivory-beige sections separated by cinched-in 'waists'. They are sold packed in moist mud, which helps keep them fresh, or washed and often vacuum-packed in supermarkets. Choose hard specimens with smooth skin unmarred by cuts or cracks.

Raw lotus root has a texture that is not unlike a very fine-grained waxy potato—crisp and dense. It has buff skin and pale ivory flesh that discolours slowly when cut. Simmered in soup, it turns an attractive pinky-beige but becomes muddy-hued if cooked for a long time. At first taste, cooked lotus root may seem quite bland. However, as you eat it, its subtly starchy character, with a rounded, nutty quality and a faint natural sweetness, grows on you.

Mud-coated lotus roots wrapped in newspaper keep for several days in the refrigerator; lightly dampen the newspaper with a spray if it dries out. Washed lotus roots, if not vacuum-packed, can be wrapped in two or three layers of paper towels, then in lightly dampened newspaper before refrigerating.

A versatile ingredient, lotus root can be eaten raw, pickled, steamed, braised, curried, stir-fried, deep-fried and even made into desserts. Choose younger, smaller specimens for pickling or brief cooking and larger, starchier ones for stewing or soup-brewing. It is a necessary ingredient in several classic Cantonese soups, for example lotus root with pork and dried cuttlefish, as well as lotus root with peanuts. Some Japanese recipes grate it into soups before a quick simmer until it is done. If you have a long chopstick and plenty of patience, you can stuff the tunnels of a lotus root section, steam or poach it whole, then slice it crossways to reveal the pattern. Some Japanese recipes use a miso-based stuffing and Chinese ones a seasoned glutinous rice stuffing. Remember to leave room for the latter to expand.

Blanched lotus root slices retain a pleasing crunch and need only a light dressing—a tangy vinaigrette, seasoned Japanese dashi stock or vinegar, perhaps

even just lime juice and a pinch of sugar—to make a great hot-weather salad or snack. *Fukujin-zuke*, a classic Japanese vegetable pickle, invariably includes lotus root.

Lotus root sections can be cut into rough chunks for braising or stewing. Briefly deep-frying the lotus root pieces beforehand brings out their nutty nuances. Try adding these to western lamb or beef stews—you may be surprised at how well the flavours combine. For an unusual side dish, try blanching lotus root chunks, then stir-frying them with butter and herbs, as you might treat potatoes, until golden brown.

India boasts many lotus root preparations. As you might expect of a region famous for lakes spilling over with lotus flowers, Kashmir is the home of a myriad lotus root dishes, whether stewed with various greens, braised in a spicy yoghurt gravy, cooked with mutton or pickled with vinegar, among many other ways. Its robust texture is valued as a meat surrogate.

Paper-thin lotus root slices can be deep-fried into disarmingly pretty chips. Sliced lotus root is also used in Chinese sweet dessert soups and can be candied by a slow simmering in syrup. In Thailand, the slices and syrup are eaten over crushed ice as a dessert.

In Chinese medicine, lotus root is a tonifying food that is good for the spleen, heart and kidneys. Raw lotus root juice cools the system and helps to alleviate bleeding.

Radishes

Common Luo bo (Mandarin), Lobak putih
(Malay), Mullangi (Tamil), Mooli (Hindi),
Daikon (Japan), Labanos (Tagalog),
Hua pak gat kao (Thai)
Botanical Raphanus sativus

Radish cultivars come in an enormous variety of shapes and sizes but among the most familiar within and outside Asia are the long, cylindrical daikon-type roots with white flesh and skin, and the slightly stubbier Chinese radishes with green flesh and skin. Slightly less common are Korean radishes, shaped like elongated eggs with all-white skin or white skin shading into green shoulders. Other radishes with coloured skin or flesh—such as the Chinese red-skinned radishes, which can be round or long, or the pretty 'beauty heart' radishes with white skins and blushing red cores—are not easy to find outside China.

The flavour of all raw radishes balances elements of sweetness, pungency and bite, as well as a subtle loamy quality. Large white radishes can vary a fair bit and unpredictably in pungency, from sweet and innocuous to quite peppery. Long, slow cooking helps to turn their sharpness into a gentle purr. Green radishes look like they might be pungent but, in fact, are often very sweet, especially when slow-braised. Small white radishes—and their greens—are more pungent than you might think but, apart from that, are quite bland.

Asian radishes should be used as soon as possible after purchase as they do not keep well. If you want to eat them raw, purchase and prepare the same day for optimum texture and flavour. Wrap them individually in plastic wrap and keep in the refrigerator's vegetable drawer until needed. Small radishes with greens attached should be used up within a day of purchase, while the greens are still fresh. Wrap the greens in slightly damp paper towels, then loosely pack roots in a large plastic bag before refrigerating.

White radishes are that rare thing, a vegetable that can be eaten and enjoyed at almost every stage of cooking, from crisply raw to almost dissolving— cut them into matchsticks or coarse shreds and stir-fry until crisp-tender; cut them into quarter-moons or rough chunks and wok-braise until sweet and only just soft enough to pierce with a chopstick; or double-boil with pork or chicken until plush and melting.

Clockwise from top: Japanese daikon with leaves; trimmed Chinese white radish; baby Chinese white radishes with leaves.and Chinese green radish.

It is perhaps in the Japanese kitchen that radishes reach their widest potential. There, it is pickled, steamed, stewed, grated raw as a condiment and transformed into many garnishes. Dipping sauces are given a kick by a spoonful of plain grated radish, or radish grated with red chillies to make rosy-tinted *momiji-oroshi* (maple leaf grate). *Oden* would be unthinkable without thick rounds of soft *furofuki* daikon and in other dishes, the rounds are topped with thickened, seasoned miso or piquant hoisin-based sauce. *Takuan*, a popular Japanese pickle, is whole daikon pickled in rice bran and tinted yellow with gardenia pods. Daikon is also preserved in sake lees to make a white, beautifully smooth and succulent pickle.

In the Korean kitchen, many kinds of kimchi use radish as an ingredient, capitalising on the various textures of different sizes of radish when sliced and salted in different ways. Dried radish, variously seasoned, is a common ingredient across China and the Chinese diaspora in Southeast Asia.

Kashmiri cuisine has an unusual raita combining yoghurt with coarsely grated radishes, chillies and spices. In Nepal, grated radish is cooked with a sprinkling of cumin, coriander and other spices, in little more than its own juices and then thickened with a little chickpea flour.

Sweet Potatoes

Common Fan shu (Mandarin), Sarkaraivalli kilangu (Tamil),
Shakarkand, Mitha alu, Ratalu (Hindi), Kamote (Tagalog),
Satsuma imo, Kansho (Japanese), Man kaeng (Thai),
Kumara (New Zealand), Boniato (south America)
Botanical Ipomoea batatas

All sweet potatoes are shaped somewhat like teardrops and tapered at both ends. This basic shape may be stretched, as seen in elongated Japanese sweet potatoes, or squashed to become fat and cuddly, like many purple sweet potatoes. While the shape of a sweet potato is an arguable clue to its identity, its skin colour is most unreliable. Many orange-, white- or yellow-fleshed sweet potatoes look the same on the outside: brown. Helpfully, the Okinawan purple sweet potato (*beni imo*) has dusty purple skin and purple flesh to match. Other Japanese purple-fleshed sweet potatoes, however, have beige skins. Still other Japanese sweet potatoes have garnet skins. The good news is that sweet potatoes are seldom mislabelled in markets and supermarkets.

Texture-wise, sweet potatoes lie on a spectrum between moist- and dry-fleshed. Those at the former extreme have a soft, damp texture after cooking and those at the latter, one crumbly and starchy. Taste-wise, they range widely from just barely sweet to extremely sugary, and from earthy and coarse to fragrant and subtle. Orange sweet potatoes often have the most 'pure' sweetness of all, while Japanese sweet potatoes (pale yellow, beige or orange flesh) can be sweet and taste like a fusion of potato and chestnut. Dry-fleshed purple sweet potatoes have an aromatic, delicate savour that is strangely but definitely reminiscent of lychee. Seldom seen in Asia, white-fleshed south American types tend to be less sweet and more starchy.

Do not keep these roots enclosed in a bag or in the refrigerator as they will sprout or spoil. Store in a wire or rattan basket at cool room temperature, in a well ventilated place away from direct sunlight, and use within a few days.

Sweet potatoes at peak freshness are best appreciated simply steamed or baked and eaten plain. For a smooth mash, steam them over high heat, then peel. For a drier, more solid texture, bake at 200°C (400°F) from a cold-oven start until tender. Never boil them as they will leak vitamins, flavour and colour.

Sweet potato skins are edible, though mostly not as tasty as regular potato skins. You can cook and serve sweet potatoes in every way you would treat a regular potato: baked and topped with butter, sautéed, roasted and mashed. They can be used to top casseroles and pies, mashed for croquettes and patties and fried into chips or crisps. However, the individuality of different flesh-colour types open up a wider world of possibilities. Here is a concise, but certainly not exhaustive, list of flavour compatibilities.

Clockwise from top, left: Beniazuma Japanese yellow sweet potatoes; purple sweet potatoes; white sweet potatoes; orange sweet potatoes and Harukogane Japanese yellow sweet potatoes.

Orange goes well with citrus, cumin, olive oil, garlic, ginger, onions, sweet spices like cinnamon and clove, brown sugar, coriander seeds and leaves, chilli, raisins, peanuts, sesame seeds, most meats, dried and fresh prawns (shrimps) and salty cheeses.

Purple goes well with all forms of coconut, lychees, longans, rosewater, vanilla, ginger, seafood, cream sauces, miso, chestnuts, Chinese sausage, duck, pork and sticky rice.

Yellow goes well with chestnuts, apples, raisins, vanilla, lemon, ginger, cream, pork, beef, pumpkin, miso, cream and salty cheeses, onions and leeks.

Sweet potatoes are rich in antioxidants, fibre and calcium. Orange and yellow varieties contain beta-carotene: purple ones are laden with anthocyanins, which bleed readily into the water if you boil them, and in fact may have the highest levels of antioxidant activity out of all sweet potatoes. In Chinese medicine, sweet potatoes are a spleen and kidney tonic and a reliable source of yin energy, which helps to lubricate the internal organs.

Taro

Common Taro potato, Yu tou (Mandarin), Keladi
(Malay), Sato imo (Japanese), Seppan kilangu
(Tamil), Arvi (Hindi), Pheuak (Thai),
Gabi (Tagalog)
Botanical Colocasia esculenta

Large taro corms sold in Asian markets are typically about 30 cm (12 in) long.
Some are shaped like barrels and others like rugby balls, with more tapered
ends. Baby taro are round or oval and small enough for you to fit one or two in
your palm. Both have skins that are dark brown, rough and ringed with ridges.
Raw taro flesh is mainly white or cream in colour and may be flecked with
brown, pink or purple. Choose taro that are as unblemished as possible, and
without a sour or fermented odour or mould.

Cooked taro has a starchy solidity reminiscent of both potato and sweet
potato and is easy to mash because its starch granules are tiny compared to other
root vegetables. It has a mild, rich sweetness that is very faintly reminiscent
of chestnut, coconut and macadamia nuts and, thus, has affinities for these
ingredients. Cooked taro is a lavender-grey hue, while cooked purple taro is an
attractive violet. Small corms are smoother and more moist to the point of being
slightly sticky, while larger corms are starchier and more crumbly.

Keep taro at cool room temperature, in a well-ventilated place out of
direct sunlight. Use it up as soon as possible after purchase. Taro is best peeled
before cooking.

To the Asian palate, taro is a more soulful ingredient than potato, with
more depth and versatility. It is adaptable to both savoury and sweet uses and
can take on a wide variety of textures, from dense and meaty to creamy and
smooth to crisp and crunchy. It is also able to hold its own alongside other
strongly-flavoured ingredients.

In Chinese cuisine, taro is often steamed and mashed, and then cooked
a second time, for example in *wu gok* (deep-fried stuffed taro croquettes), *orh
nee* (sweetened taro purée with gingko nuts and lard) and deep-fried rings

of mashed taro used as 'baskets' for stir-fries. It is often paired with pork or duck, as seen in deboned duck spread with taro paste and deep-fried, or pork belly stewed with taro. Halved peeled baby taro make fine additions to a slow-cooked stew, and their sticky juices will help thicken the gravy.

Taro chunks or mashed taro make a satisfying meat substitute due to their starchy texture, and are often used as such in Asian vegetarian cuisine. Combine taro mash with crumbled cotton tofu and dried shiitake mushrooms that have been cooked

Clockwise from top, left: Mature taro; slice of mature taro; medium-size taro; baby taro and young taro.

and finely chopped, then use the mixture as a base for croquettes, patties, or 'sausages' wrapped in soy bean skin. Cubed taro can be cooked in biryanis or pilafs in place of meat chunks, and will add its own special fragrance to the rice.

Push steamed baby taro through a sieve while still warm to get a very fine mash, then dilute it to a pouring consistency with white sauce, cream or soy bean milk and use it as a binding sauce for vegetable gratins. This sauce is especially good if seasoned with a little white or yellow miso. Thinly sliced or shredded taro becomes very crunchy when deep-fried until golden. Sprinkle with plain sea salt and black pepper, gomashio (Japanese sesame salt) or Indian chaat masala spice mixture for a great snack to go with drinks.

NOTE: Taro contains oxalic acid crystals that may irritate the skin upon contact. Wear gloves when preparing it to avoid this risk. Some people who are allergic to yams and taro may feel a prickling sensation in their throats when they eat them. Always cook taro fully. Like true yams, taro contains oxalic acid crystals which may irritate hands or throats upon contact. To avoid this, wear gloves when preparing it, and cook it fully before consumption.

Turnips

Common Wu jing (Chinese), Kabu (Japanese),
Nool khol (Tamil), Shalgam (Hindi)
Botanical Brassica rapa

Turnip roots originated from northern Europe but spread to China and from there, to Japan and the rest of Asia at least a millennium ago. They range fairly widely in size and shape, from spherical to ovoid to long and thin. Baby turnips can be as small as ping-pong balls, while the large ones can weigh approximately 1 kg (2 lb 3 oz). Most common varieties are white-fleshed with skins that are all white or white flushed with red, pink or purple. Less widely available hybrids may have red or yellow skins.

Some of the most attractive turnips can be found in Japan. Kokabu turnips, for instance, are so very white and symmetrical that they look like cartoon buns. Hinona kabu turnips are long and tapered, with vivid purple-pink shoulders; they are used for making pink pickles.

The flavour of turnips (often maligned in England as dank and gas-inducing) sometimes seems to combine the sweetness of radishes with the ghostly pungency of cabbage stalks. Stick to young, small, fresh turnips to avoid the risk of less than pleasant flavour nuances. Texture-wise, turnips are much like radishes—crisp when raw; crunchy and pliable when salted and pickled; and smooth and buttery-soft when slow-cooked.

Wrap turnips in plastic wrap or resealable plastic bags, then refrigerate but use them up within one or two days, before they dry out and become acrid.

Overcooked and underseasoned turnips are an abomination, but small, fresh specimens combined with judicious accompaniments are anything but blah. Shred or slice raw turnips and salt them to remove excess water or soak them in water to make them super-crunchy, then add them to salads: they suit sweet-salty-sour-pungent Thai and Vietnamese salad dressings well.

In the Middle East, turnips may be braised with dates or date syrup, and indeed this vegetable takes well to sweet flavours. Follow the French fashion and sauté small peeled turnips with butter, sugar and salt until golden and sticky; or cut them into thin sticks and mix with cream, then sprinkle with cheese and bake into a golden gratin. Halve or quarter peeled small turnips, then toss with unsalted butter, sea salt and a dash of honey before oven-roasting at 200°C (400°F), stirring often, until brown and caramelised.

Like radishes, turnips are delicious in long-simmered meat stews or soups as they absorb the meat juices to become plump and flavourful. On the flip side, they can also be quickly stir-fried with aromatics (such as garlic, onion, Chinese or western smoked bacon and dried shrimp) and /or punchy condiments (such as chilli oil, XO sauce, Sichuan peppercorns and sesame oil).

From top: Teardrop Indian turnips and Japanese kokabu turnips.

Turnips go well with most red meats. India's Moghul cuisine esteems turnips as a winter vegetable, with one of its most famous preparations being mutton braised with turnips and saffron. Kashmir, in particular, is feted for its turnip recipes. Pakistan boasts a traditional dish called shabdeg, which slowly cooks turnips and lamb or chicken together until both are meltingly tender.

Turnip pickles, typically tinted a vivid pink from beet slices, are an essential pantry staple in Egyptian, Lebanese and Syrian households, where they are served as side dishes. Japanese cooks pickle turnips in brine in a very similar way, and Koreans make a water kimchi of turnips in which the cool pickling liquid is drunk as well.

Ube

Common Purple yam, Violet yam,
Perumvalli kilangu (Tamil), Kham alu (Hindi)
Botanical Dioscorea alata

Ube yams look unimpressive on the outside, being irregularly lumpy and covered with greyish-brown and typically dusty skin. Slice into one, however, and you will reveal flesh of a beautiful violet-purple hue, which can be so intense it practically glows. Despite their difference in colour, purple yams are cultivars of the same species as white yams.

Cooked ube has a meaty, moist texture, with a nutty, savoury quality. The cooking process deepens its colour to a rich royal purple.

Store ube yams in a cool, well ventilated place out of direct sunlight and cook within a few days of purchase, while still firm. They are usually fairly misshapen, so chop the washed yams into large pieces before removing the skin with a sharp knife. There are likely to be woody, soft or discoloured spots, so carve these out at the same time.

It is best to steam ube chunks over high heat until soft before mashing. Boiling it leaches out the colour, so avoid this. In savoury dishes, ube takes well to beef, duck and lamb and mashed ube makes a tasty base for fish or minced meat croquettes. In general, you can substitute it for potato and taro in preparations that feature those.

Ube is an important staple in the Philippines; a local cultivar called *kinampay* is considered to have the best flavour. In the Filipino kitchen, ube is used to make stews, braised dishes, custards, ice creams, mousses, jam, steamed and baked cakes, chips, breads, sweets, muffins and turnover fillings.

Try adding cubed steamed ube to Malay sweets, such as *bubur cha cha*, *pengat* or even ice *kacang*. Ube has a natural partner in all forms of coconut, as evidenced by Filipino desserts like ube and *macapuno* (young jelly coconut flesh) cake, ube and coconut cream custard, and so on. You may be able to find dried ube powder in Filipino provision shops. This can be reconstituted for use in desserts that require fresh ube, though it does not have the full fragrance of the fresh yam.

Like purple sweet potatoes, ube's bright colour stems from anthocyanin pigments, which are also powerful antioxidant compounds.

NOTE: This is a true yam, containing oxalic acid crystals that may irritate the skin upon contact. Wear gloves when preparing it to avoid this risk. Some people who are allergic to true yams may feel a prickling sensation in their throats when they eat them.

Wasabi

Common Shan yu cai, Shan kui (Mandarin)
Botanical Wasabia japonica, Eutrema japonica

Cylindrical wasabi rhizomes can grow up to 20 cm (8 cm) long and about 3 cm (1^1/$_4$ in) across. They are clad in ridged, knobbly, greenish-brown skin that is sometimes flecked with dark brown or black. Underneath the skin is light green flesh that fades to almost white at the core. Wasabi should be sold and bought with at least a few heart-shaped leaves still sprouting from its crown, a sign of freshness.

Grown on streambeds, wasabi requires cold, clean running water as a growing environment. Demanding and difficult to cultivate, it is, thus, typically very expensive. This also means that the majority of what is sold as wasabi, whether in powder or paste form, is horseradish spiked with food colouring. In fact, if it is in any form other than a fresh root, you can be virtually certain it is fake wasabi. Observe the two side by side and the difference is apparent. Real grated wasabi is a pale apple-green with miniscule dark flecks, while fake wasabi is often an oddly vivid green.

The difference in flavour is even more stark. Real wasabi has a light, floral delicacy that slowly shades into a soft heat, and fades away over a few seconds. In comparison, fake wasabi is acrid, searing and persistent, neither complex nor seductive. Unlike the mainly mouth-searing effect of chilli, the heat of real wasabi is felt as much in the sinuses as on the tongue, rather like mustard. Fake wasabi, which often contains mustard to mimic this effect, amplifies this to crude levels.

The volatile fragrance of fresh wasabi means that it should be grated just before use, and it is best eaten uncooked. Traditionally in Japan, it is reduced to a fine purée on a rough grater made of sharkskin. Ceramic or metal graters are acceptable (and affordable) substitutes. Pare off the skin before grating but do not pare beyond what you mean to grate. Once you are done, wrap the remaining root in slightly damp paper towels, and then in plastic wrap, and store it in the refrigerator. Try to use up a fresh root while it is still firm and juicy.

Apart from its irreplaceable role next to sashimi and sushi, try adding grated fresh wasabi to vinaigrettes, simple sauces made of white meat or seafood pan juices and vegetable-juice sauces or dressings. Simply spoon it over or toss it with a dish as a final fillip just before serving: for example, add a dash of wasabi to spaghetti with white wine and clams. Wasabi goes well with other subtle flavours, especially seafood, and should not be overwhelmed with excessive spice or fermented flavours.

Because of its brute strength, fake wasabi does have its uses, notably in rich dishes with enough fat to blunt our tastebuds' acuity. For example, fake wasabi works better than the real thing in wasabi mayonnaise, a popular salad dressing or dip in modern Chinese and Japanese restaurants, because its stridency cuts through the mayonnaise's oil and egg. Likewise, fake wasabi is useful for flavouring cream sauces, oil-based marinades, mashed potatoes and such. Try serving meats traditionally eaten with horseradish with wasabi instead—roast beef sandwiches with wasabi mayonnaise or roast pork with wasabi mashed potatoes.

Japanese supermarket sushi counters sometimes sell wasabi rhizomes or leaves pickled in sake lees, a delicacy from Shizuoka. These can be eaten on their own or used as a condiment to season dressings and sauces.

Wasabi's pungency comes from compounds called isothiocyanates, whose medical abilities are slowly being unveiled by research. Results indicate that wasabi has anti-microbial powers, which shed light on its traditional association with raw fish, and may also be beneficial in treating tooth decay, controlling blood clotting and preventing cancer.

Water Chestnuts

Common Ma ti (Mandarin), Singhara (Tamil, Hindi),
Haeo (Thai), Ino kuro guwai (Japanese), Apulid (Tagalog)
Botanical Eleocharis dulcis

Water chestnuts are flattened little corms about the size of golf balls. Covered by shiny black skins, each traced by a few ridges and some brown frills, the flesh underneath is white and juicy. Choose hard and heavy specimens when purchasing and absolutely avoid those with soft spots. For the sake of convenience, choose rounder ones as these are easier to peel.

The succulent crunch and sweet flavour of fresh water chestnuts—like the best possible fusion of Chinese pear, apple and baby sweetcorn kernels—is inimitable. There is little point to cooking them until these qualities are completely lost, so keep cooking times brief.

When it comes to water chestnuts, always buy a little more than you need as peeling and trimming inevitably decimates your quantity. If grown in dirty water, water chestnuts may pose a food hygiene risk, so make sure you wash them very well before preparing and eating them. Rinse with boiling water, if necessary.

Store cleaned water chestnuts in the refrigerator, immersed in clean water in an airtight container; they will keep this way for a few days. Peel them only just before they are needed and use a paring knife rather than a vegetable peeler, which will clog. Cut away all browned areas and smell each one to confirm it is fresh; you may find the odd fermented one, which will smell slightly of alcohol.

To enjoy water chestnuts at their simplest—peel them, rinse, then chill until very cold and eat au naturel; or juice them and drink the juice over ice. You can also gild the lily by soaking them in jasmine-scented water or drizzling over screwpine (pandan)-flavoured syrup. A cooling Chinese drink is made by boiling diced water chestnuts with rock sugar; a little water chestnut starch can be used to thicken this into a sweet soup.

Coarsely diced raw water chestnuts add crunch to all manner of salads and dips: tuna mayonnaise, sour cream and clam dip, sliced oranges and red onions dressed with olive oil, chicken salad, Chinese jellyfish salad, mixed-sprout medleys, Thai salads based on grilled beef or pork or minced meat larb mixtures. Try slipping thin slices into a club sandwich or into delicate tea sandwiches of smoked ham or fish.

Stir finely diced or chopped water chestnuts into minced meat or minced seafood mixtures before steaming or deep-frying. Smash or chop them to add to soup broths, whether to be simmered quickly or double-boiled slowly, or toss them whole or halved into stir-fries.

Water chestnut flour, processed from the dried corms, is sometimes grittier than other cooking starches, such as corn or rice flour. Simply whizz it in a blender (food processor) for several seconds to smoothen it out. Used as a coating for deep-fried items, it produces a delicate, snowy-looking and admirably crisp finish. As a thickener, it produces lovely glossy, translucent sauces.

In traditional Chinese medicine, water chestnuts are a cooling food that help to reduce excess heat in the body that causes sore throats or fevers. They relieve indigestion and hypertension and promote urination. Ayurvedic medicine prescribes poultices of water chestnut paste for inflamed or swollen skin and recommends that the corms' juice or flesh be consumed to combat fatigue.

Yam Bean

Common Sha ge (Mandarin), Ubi sengkuang (Malay),
Bengkuang, Bangkuang (Bahasa Indonesia), Jicama
(Spanish), Man kaeo (Thai), Sinkamas (Tagalog),
Thani ootan kilangu (Tamil), Mishrikand (Hindi)
Botanical *Pachyrhizus erosus*

These roots—which have nothing to do with beans—are shaped like tops, squashed spheres with tapered bottoms. Their skin is the colour of brown envelopes. They are at their best when fresh, young and juicy. Older yam beans have thicker skins, a woodier texture and are less sweet.

Eaten raw, the crisp white flesh of the yam bean has a clean, faintly starchy flavour vaguely reminiscent of an un-sugary water chestnut. Cooked, it acquires a mellow, silken texture but also gets blander, so season it judiciously.

Yam bean's tough skin, which has a thin but strong underlayer, is best removed by a small sharp knife as even slightly blunt vegetable peelers will slip, slide and clog.

In Singapore, yam bean is best known, and perhaps best loved, as the main constituent of *popiah* filling. This recipe makes the most of the root's ability to absorb the flavours of the liquid it has been cooked in, and also its smooth texture. Brief cooking works as well as long simmering, however; try stir-frying shredded or julienned yam bean for a quick side dish. In Penang, the traditional *joo her char* stir-fries and briefly braises a combination of shredded yam bean, dried cuttlefish, carrot and pork that is eaten wrapped in lettuce leaves with sambal *belacan*. Add finely diced yam bean to minced meat patties before steaming or deep-frying to create little bursts of crunchy-tender texture.

In Latin America, yam bean is commonly eaten raw in salads or snacks and often paired with acidic or intensely-flavoured ingredients like lime, orange and chilli powder—an obvious parallel to salty and spicy Asian salads such as rojak, which also includes the root. Use finely julienned raw yam bean as a crisp, refreshing garnish for multi-textured main dishes, such as tacos, hamburgers, kebabs, sandwich wraps and so on.

The crisp blandness of yam bean makes it a good staple for pickling, whether for quick vinegar-soaked pickles like the kind served as small-

dish appetisers in Chinese restaurants or stuffed into Vietnamese baguette sandwiches, or longer-lasting Indian-type pickles.

Having a similar texture, yam bean is sometimes used as a cheap substitute for water chestnuts, for example in the Thai dessert thap thim krawp or red rubies. However, economy is really the only reason to recommend this as water chestnuts are much sweeter.

Yamaimo

Common Mountain yam, Mountain potato,
Chinese yam, Cinnamon vine, Shan yao,
huai shan (Mandarin)
Botanical Dioscorea batatas, dioscorea opposita

Yamaimo is the umbrella name for Japanese mountain yam tubers, whose various cultivars have different shapes but are very similar in texture and taste. Each has its own colloquial name: nagaimo are long and shaped like baseball bats: yamato imo and ichou imo are flattened and shaped like a whale's tail or straight with knobby ends, like bones; tsukune imo are lumpy, like misshapen round bread loaves. All have pale to dark beige skins speckled with dark brown dots and short, fuzzy hairs; inside, they are white. The fresh, hard roots are stored in sawdust, most of which is brushed off before they are packaged for sale. Fresh Chinese yam or *shan yao* (also called *huai shan* because the Huai valley is a famous source of the yam) is long and cylindrical, resembling nagaimo; it is the same species, botanically speaking.

Peeled and grated, yamaimo has a sticky, mucus-like consistency beloved by the Japanese. Sliced and cooked, it loses its sliminess and acquires a starchy, yam-like texture. It has a bland, cassava-like taste, with a faint edge of pungency reminiscent of radishes.

If yamaimo is to be eaten raw, soak it in a mixture of two parts water and one part vinegar for a short while to neutralise the oxalate. Grated raw yamaimo seasoned with dashi stock becomes *tororo*, which the Japanese dollop onto soba, rice or sashimi tuna. *Tororo* is also eaten plain, garnished with seaweed and water-shield leaves. Unseasoned grated yamaimo is often used as a binding agent for deep-fried or pan-fried foods, and it does this impressively well—a single tablespoon being enough to bind about one cup of minced meat or grated vegetables. Pre-mixed *okonomiyaki* (savoury pancake) flour often contains dried yamaimo starch. To pound yamaimo into a fine paste for making *tororo* or for use as a binder, the traditional tools are a Japanese *suribachi* (ridged ceramic mortar) and *surikogi* (pestle). Modern laser-cut, square-toothed rasp graters also do a good job. Old-fashioned box graters are not sharp enough to cope with its stickiness. If you only have a box grater, freezing the yamaimo beforehand helps to reduce the mess, but also makes it harder to grate.

Raw yamaimo can be cut into strips and tossed with zestily flavoured condiments as a foil for its blandness, for example natto (fermented soy beans) or seasoned rice vinegar. The Japanese also grill peeled sections of yamaimo, then braise them in seasoned stock until tender. Grated yamaimo can be mixed with water or stock, then poured into a bowl and steamed into a thick, custardy side dish.

In the Chinese kitchen, Chinese yam is most often seen as chalk-white slices of the dried tuber, a frequent inclusion in traditional Chinese herbal blends. Pre-packaged herb combinations for brewing soup or steaming with chicken invariably include dried Chinese yam. Peeled chunks of the fresh tuber can also be simmered in soups and stews, where it will take on a dense but tender consistency. It is mild enough to partner most meats but does not shine next to seafood.

Clockwise from top, left: Japanese nagaimo; fresh Chinese yam (*shan yao*); Japanese yamato imo and slices of dried *shan yao*.

Among the compounds this yam contains is allantoin, which aids the healing of tissues, and inulin, a soluble fibre. In traditional Chinese medicine, Chinese yam is a very important source of yin energy and is prescribed for diabetes, diarrhoea and other disorders. A common ingredient in herbal mixtures for soups and tonics, it is a sweet and neutral food that strengthens the stomach and spleen, and is a lung and kidney tonic.

NOTE: This is a true yam, containing oxalic acid crystals that may irritate the skin upon contact. Wear gloves when preparing it to avoid this risk. When eaten raw, yamaimo may cause a prickling sensation in the throats of people with yam allergies.

Stir-fried Chicken with Holy Basil Serves 4

Cooking oil *2 Tbsp*

Garlic *4 cloves, peeled and coarsely pounded*

Chilli padi *4, coarsely pounded*

Coriander root *30 g, coarsely pounded*

Black peppercorns *1/2 tsp, coarsely pounded*

Chicken *500 g (1 lb 1 1/2 oz), deboned and sliced*

Palm sugar (gula Melaka) *2 tsp, grated*

Fish sauce *2 Tbsp*

Holy basil leaves *85 g (3 oz)*

1. Heat oil and sauté the pounded garlic, chilli padi, coriander root and black peppercorns until aromatic.

2. Add the chicken slices and the rest of the ingredients. Stir-fry for about 10 minutes, until the chicken is cooked.

3. Dish out and serve hot.

Stir-fried Sweet Potato Leaves Serves 3-4

Chicken breasts *2, skinned and cut into small dice*

Chinese dried mushrooms *10, soaked or briefly boiled in water to soften, trimmed of hard stalks and caps quartered*

Dried longan flesh *50 g (2 oz), rinsed and drained*

Water *1 litre (32 fl oz / 4 cups)*

Salt *$1/2$ tsp*

Ground black pepper *$1/2$ tsp + extra for garnishing (optional)*

1. Pour boiling water over the sweet potato leaves and let stand for 1–2 minutes to rid the leaves of any sap.

2. Drain water and rinse the leaves with cold water to prevent the leaves from overcooking. Chop up the leaves.

3. Heat the oil and fry the dried prawns until aromatic. Add the pounded chillies and garlic. Stir-fry for 1 minute.

4. Add the blanched sweet potatoes leaves and the rest of the ingredients. Stir-fry over high heat for about 15 minutes or until the dish is dry.

5. Dish out and serve as a side dish.

Grilled Lemon Basil Chicken Wings Makes 10

Lemon basil leaves *85 g (3 oz),*
coarsely pounded

Garlic *8 cloves, peeled and*
coarsely pounded

Plum sauce *200 ml*

Light soy sauce *125 ml (4 fl oz /*
1/2 cup)

Cider vinegar *85 ml (2 1/2 fl oz /*
1/3 cup)

Hoisin sauce *100 ml (3 1/2 fl oz)*

Honey *85 ml (2 1/2 fl oz / 1/3 cup)*

Sesame oil *2 tsp*

Chicken wings *20*

1. Combine all the ingredients except the chicken wings in a large bowl. Mix well. Add the chicken wings and mix until well coated.

2. Place the marinated chicken wings into an airtight container and keep refrigerated overnight or for at least 6 hours.

3. Preheat the oven to 180°C.

4. Drain the chicken wings from the marinade and arrange on a wire rack placed on a baking tray. Reserve the marinade for basting.

5. Bake the chicken wings for 40 minutes, basting the chicken wings occasionally with the marinade.

Note: Instead of roasting the chicken wings in the oven, you can also barbecue them. Alternatively you can use other parts of the chicken such as chicken thighs, drumsticks or chicken breasts.

Otak Otak Serves 6

Galangal 3-cm (1¼-in) knob, skinned

Fresh turmeric 2-cm (³/₄-in) knob, skinned

Candlenuts 8

Lemon grass 2 stalks, sliced

Shallots 10, peeled

Garlic 4 cloves, peeled

Dried chillies 30, soaked to soften and drained

Coconut cream 125 ml (4 fl oz / ½ cup)

Spanish mackerel fillet 750 g (1 lb 11 oz), minced

Salt 1 tsp or to taste

Rice flour 2 tsp

Corn flour (cornstarch) 1 Tbsp

Sugar 2 tsp

Eggs 2, lightly beaten

Kaffir lime leaves 6, finely shredded

Banana leaves as needed, cut into 20 x 18-cm (8 x 7-in) pieces, softened by steaming or scalding in hot water

1. Grind the galangal, turmeric, candlenuts, lemongrass, shallots garlic, dried chillies and coconut cream until smooth. Pour into a mixing bowl.

2. Add the remaining ingredients, except for the banana leaves, to the bowl and mix well.

3. Spoon 3–4 Tbsp of the mixture onto a banana leaf. Form a parcel by folding the two long sides over to enclose the mixture and folding the short ends. Secure with staples or toothpicks. Repeat until the mixture is used up.

4. Alternatively, place the mixture in a greased casserole dish.

5. Steam for 20 minutes or until the mixture is firm.

Note: Instead of using only minced fish, you may want to keep 150 g (5⅓ oz) of the fish and dice it to give the *otak otak* more bite. The *otak otak* can also be made with a mixture of minced prawns, squid and fish.

Baked Taro Cake Serves 6

Peeled taro *550 g (1 lb 3¹/₂ oz)*

Coconut cream *150 ml (5 fl oz), mixed with 150 ml (5 fl oz) water*

Plain (all-purpose) flour *30 g (1 oz)*

Palm sugar (gula melaka) *220 g (8 oz), grated*

Eggs *5, lightly beaten*

Salt *¹/₂ tsp*

Crisp-fried shallots *1 Tbsp, crushed*

1. Divide taro into 150 g (5¹/₃ oz) and 400 g (14¹/₃ oz) portions. Dice smaller portion, then steam both portions until cooked. Mash larger portion and set both aside.

2. Combine coconut cream, flour and palm sugar in a mixing bowl. Stir until sugar is dissolved, then strain and set aside.

3. Strain beaten eggs into a large bowl. Mix in mashed taro, salt and crisp-fried shallots and beat until smooth.

4. Combine coconut cream, mashed taro mixture and diced taro in a pot. Cook over low heat, stirring constantly, until slightly thickened. Remove from heat.

5. Preheat oven to 180°C (350°F).

6. Grease a 25 x 4-cm (10 x 2-in) rectangular cake pan and pour taro mixture into pan, spreading it out evenly.

7. Bake for 25 minutes or until golden brown on top. Set aside to cool thoroughly before cutting into squares to serve.

8. For an alternative presentation, use 20 small metal cups instead of the cake pan and reduce the baking time to 15 minutes.

Taro Croquettes Serves 5

Wheat starch flour (tang meen fun) 60 g (2 oz)

Boiling hot water 100 ml (3¹/₂ fl oz)

Taro 500 g (1 lb 1¹/₂ oz), steamed until soft, then mashed

Dried prawns (shrimps) 30 g (1 oz), soaked for 20 minutes, then drained and finely chopped

Dried shiitake mushrooms 5, soaked for 20 minutes, then drained, stems discarded and finely chopped

Chinese sausage 1, diced

Finely chopped spring onions (scallions) 2 Tbsp

Finely chopped Chinese chives 1 Tbsp

Salt 1 tsp

Light soy sauce 2 Tbsp

Castor sugar 1 tsp

Ground white pepper ¹/₄ tsp

Sesame oil 1 tsp

Cornflour 150 g (5¹/₃ oz)

Cooking oil for deep-frying

1. Place wheat starch flour in a small bowl. Pour boiling hot water over and mix into a soft, sticky dough. Transfer to a large mixing bowl.

2. Add all remaining ingredients, except cornflour and oil to the mixing bowl, and mix into a soft dough. Shape mixture into egg-size croquettes.

3. Heat oil for deep-frying.

4. Coat croquettes in cornflour and deep-fry until golden brown.

5. Remove with a slotted spoon and drain on absorbent paper towels. Serve hot.

Cassava Chips Serves 4

Cassava (tapioca) *300 g (11 oz)*
Ground turmeric *½ tsp*
Chilli powder *1 tsp*
Fine salt *½ tsp*
Cooking oil *for deep-frying*

1. Peel cassava and cut crossways into wafer-thin slices.

2. Combine turmeric, chilli powder and salt in a large bowl and mix well. Add cassava slices and toss until they are well coated.

3. Heat the oil for deep-frying and deep-fry the cassava slices in small batches for 2–3 minutes. Stir often so the slices will brown evenly and float to the surface.

4. Use a slotted spoon to remove the chips from the oil and drain on absorbent paper towels.

5. Allow chips to cool thoroughly before storing in an airtight container.

Note: Use relatively tender cassava to make these chips because older or more mature roots contain more sugar and the chips will be sweet. Weigh whole cassavas to determine their maturity and use only those that weigh about 750 g (1 lb 11 oz) for this recipe. For variation, finely chop 3 sprigs of curry leaves and toss them together with raw cassava chips and seasoning ingredients before deep-frying. The curry leaves become deeply aromatic when fried and impart a certain zing to the chips. Do not reuse the oil used to fry the cassava chips because the starch that would have leached into the oil causes it to develop an undesirable flavour and odour, and to go rancid rapidly.

Raspberry Wine Jellies Makes 12 pieces

Fresh raspberries *200 g (7 oz)*
Zinfandel rosé wine *750 ml (24 fl oz / 3 cups)*
Castor sugar *125 g (4^1/$_2$ oz)*
Konnyaku jelly powder *1^1/$_4$ tsp*

1. Rinse raspberries gently and place them on a plate lined with absorbent paper towels to drain for a few minutes. Divide them among 12 small jelly moulds and set aside.

2. Pour wine into a non-stick saucepan and set over medium-low heat. Whisk sugar and jelly powder together, then slowly add to wine, stirring constantly with a whisk until jelly dissolves and liquid comes to a gentle boil.

3. Still stirring constantly, simmer wine mixture for 3–4 minutes or until foam starts to subside and no specks of undissolved powder are visible.

4. Working as quickly as possible, fill the prepared jelly moulds with the wine mixture and tap each one to make sure there are no trapped air bubbles.

5. Let moulds stand until completely cooled, then cover with plastic wrap and refrigerate for at least 1 hour. Serve chilled and consume wihin the day.

About the Authors

Celebrity chef, cookbook author, food columnist, cooking instructor and entrepreneur, **Devagi Sanmugam** is one of Singapore's most dynamic and talented food personalities. Starting as a cooking instructor more than 20 years ago, Devagi has since built an impressive portfolio including writing more than a dozen cookbooks. She continues to innovate, being constantly involved in developing and testing original recipes for food companies, restaurants and magazines. Widely known as the Spice Queen of Singapore, Devagi has also hosted a number of television cooking shows for local and foreign media.

Christopher Tan is a writer, food consultant and author. A contributor of articles, photographs and recipes to international periodicals such as America's *Saveur* magazine and Singapore's *The Peak* and *G* magazines, he is also a food columnist for Singapore's *Sunday Times*. Chris regularly conducts talks, demonstrations and cooking classes on cuisine and culture at venues which have included Singapore's National History Museum and Peranakan Museum, the Sydney International Food Festival, the Musée Quai Branly in Paris, and the Culinary Institute of America. He has authored, co-authored, styled photos for and edited many cookbooks.